AIM AT THE CENTAUR STEALING YOUR WIFE

JENNIFER NELSON

UGLY DUCKLING PRESSE
BROOKLYN, NEW YORK
2015

NICCOLO PAGANINI'S *VARIATIONS ON A THEME FROM ROSSINI'S* MOSES IN EGYPT

STOP

The only way left to be radical in the United States
Creep like light on a shitty
disco ball in a bar's back room
An experimental theater
Imagine no one passing
In World of Warcraft my hippogryph
beats like maracas
I have arrived in the heart of the night elf kingdoms
I enchant weapons as a zen master scribe

BLUE AND GOLD

I break my own heart with regular travel
and no one else's ever again
a train outspeeds a tourbus in a German river valley
it very spackling rains
clouds thin over purple
meadows through permeable
roofs of hunting lodges
and well-mounted many-
pointed stags
give waterclocks the time
Caspar David Friedrich secret
hater of fog
paints a traffic circle silver green
my children build houses and sell them to trees
after the landslide a feast for ferns
no one left to die
I never explain my inmost
joy in translation
remember the party when Hölderlin proposed
planting business cards on the tourist
trail behind his tower
when the train begins a curve I finally see the future
how could I not live in the half-hacked mountains
deciding what fields
give oxygen or die
a small rusty mill
                        for long years I lived by this rusty
mill in a wood in a fearsome house
half-concrete half-timbered
I honored woodsheds and their tin covers
after all the humans had died

I won a few awards for decor
just as Italians trusted stars
to form no patterns on church ceilings
I celebrate the blue and gold way to end thought
behold the fearsome notional night
sky
copied from any
church sky a secret
consoler of Renaissance man
I remain an assistant in order to paint it
blue and gold prophylactic of reason
now some kilometers south of Jena

DON'T BELIEVE IN SUFFERING

Yeah don't believe in suffering
I have gathered among you to learn about synecdoche
How to make the interface do what I expect
The avenues in Jackson Heights
sound like it's rained all night
resenting
morning
No powerful metaphors per se but powerful
abdications, machinations
Let who pull the strings
The last month of roses
I monitor
The planes are lowering into LaGuardia
One bird just started gunning the dawn
What I mean is we should be willing to kill it

DON'T BELIEVE IN SUFFERING

Let me tell you the secret of my happiness
All the Furies at once
I linger planning murder / spontaneity
is just the overcoat of anger
that's old
Let's be real about the wait
In this fantasy once
it was okay to be poor
not because it was right but because
there wasn't a right
That red crescent moon
over the construction
cranes on Manhattan
Engels of History
It's important to be neutral here
As moralists
Neighbors
How do they know what angle
to point the dishes
Thank God that's not morality
I founded an alternative called Praise B
For example I say Thank you, Christine
for hope-bombing me
I know you mostly aren't Christine
Still
No slogan
We are moar free

THE FUTURE. VERGIL THE ENCHANTER

Facts are no longer important
Let's keep futures in the present tense
Where we see the rise of math and science
education as earnings potential
or sometimes straight up capital

and the corresponding decline
of the humanities and even
the social sciences as ghostly
shells awaiting their animus
from algorithmic population

desire has inevitably fueled
a subtle recommendation
engine
            and
we like it   We welcome

the rebirth of rhetoric
Like Montaigne my children
speak Latin
and live on a farm

Or is that Vergil

In the basket
outside the window in the engraving
by Lucas van Leyden

is tomorrow's magician

My little *Debris*[1]
My little *Chaos*[2]
My little *Awry*[3]

Gather your sandals
before a bot browses you

There's a princess's vagina
on fire in the agora

Assemble what torches you're able
We must light and heat our walls

---

[1] To be pronounced "*deb*-riss."

[2] To be pronounced "tchouse" (rhymes with *house*).

[3] To be pronounced "aw-ree."

THE MANTEGNA OCULUS RIFT

It's crude to claim our technology
moralizes that of the past: inside the a/c
remains in fact the daughter
of the emperor I have conquered
blowing down my neck

and I am a man. When we reach the next level
there are too many guns to be good:
the avatar glows ever more colors
the more essences absorbed
till the diphthong grows unpronounceable.

The whole thing's about mixing incommensurate scales.
When I tell you I'm working on measurement
remember universal means colonial,
please. Our only hope is being open to respect.
Mantegna painted his famous ceiling

oculus in Mantua in a bedroom
for people who are married, i.e.,
building on their difference.
So in my jpg of the oculus
I'm less into the Moor

or staring at a putto's well-foreshortened
balls-and-peen and more
into imitating his neighborling
who bites a marble bow
and pierces the oculus rim.

I am thinking of the people who suffer
to make my electricity possible
not out of love, because it is crude
to fall in love with the fallen
emperor's daughter, but because another

foreshortening is always possible to render another
space that dilates failure:
near the core of Mantegna's oculus
a dark slit could actually hold an eye
and probably was for hanging something. I

don't want to look it up. I love the dark navel
in the dark tear at the edge of a cloud,
fresh, I love the peacock watching it,
I love the dirty tape that crosses over it from old
conservators. When I play video games

my avatar is always a woman
and I never simulate our wars,
i.e., those of the United States: instead
on "the shattered world known as Outland," and in general
I prefer the aftermath of history

understood with fantastical consequence.
In many cities in Europe you have no choice
but even in the States I open
windows in the heat and work beside
birds, children, sirens, thunder

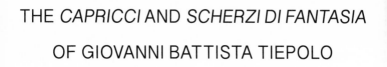

THE *CAPRICCI* AND *SCHERZI DI FANTASIA*

OF GIOVANNI BATTISTA TIEPOLO

THE ETCHERS' MERIDIAN

I have come upon Curmalmar teaching my angels

to erase the landscape: the top

of the pyramid first

then the dry

pinion of

the witch

tree, then

the entire pile
of antiquities
goes white

except one fading trumpet

But I have come for the trumpet of fire
I am ready to sing to the snake
I am Gian
Battista Tiepolo and I
have cracked an unlined globe

onto an inevitable foreground

NO PEACE AT THE COST OF MEMORY

When I saw Curmalmar touching my angels
I became the roaming meridian
destroyer and preserver
the acid and
the wax

DEATH'S FEET

the most famous huddle the godhuddle on
the Sistine ceiling
we recapitulated it
a huddle
as Death held court

Death didn't
have a throne he
sprawled on old scrolls
and corpse wrappers he
had boatlike scoliosis
and used his naked
metatarsals
to hold our various pages
he had a friendly
reading voice

someone in the huddle
thought she was a martyr but her martyr
frond was ridiculous
more like a tree
that she used ostensibly
to answer Death's hulled back

he kept the best still life hung above us
with skulls war trophies and a few
chapbooks from antiquity

Death's dog wore a mantle of its own mange
and genteelly interceded

Tiepolo left crappy
graffiti on the lectern
slash tombstone he tried
to cross out the cracks
on the face he got
moss on the knocker
right

when I lean down
he makes me
seduce Death's toes the fleshly
part of him
thrusting my pegleg
or is that my staff
both prove I am human
and have been in love
thank god my beautiful
girlfriend the martyr
holds me back

FOR THE CHILDLIKE EMPRESS

the shepherd forced
to kneel to his flock
two magicians
project their faces onto urns
panoptically
inspecting his abdication whether
cattle can ever be sovereign the boy
protects the enchanted prods
in their enchanted quiver he sees
the same thing dead Bucephalus sees
the future of all cattle ancient
horses sink like Artax into peat a softer earth
made of awkward
beginnings of writing Tië
Tië Tië Tië Tiepolo
as if with the weaker
hand still learning
enchanted script in reverse

remember children
always hate
forced tribute the magician
with power is the one with half a face
speaking an epaulette
bearded in drapery
sounded at elbow
through a trumpet by no one

the boy turns darkly to sunrise the golden
the golden-eyed ruler of wishes

TIEPOLO AS PUNCHINELLO

my handsome dark
disciples sprawl
against another naked
boy who plays a statue
in Fellini's Satyricon
porn they sprawl
on a pile of trophies war
porn I spell
it out and show I am the demon
I accuse with my nose
I push the drape aside one manly
disciple's knee
as I erase it
my urn inhales his armpit

when you drop
a sword on a wing'd
helmet right it comes to life
a blade-nosed monster you have seen
the posters of Bosch

and on that nose my owl lights
and on the urn a horse's mouth
and on the tomb Bucephalus
accuses me how
do I know he was real I answer

I draw women and steal men for love of Alexander
behind him the usual witch tree leans a would-be
cloth of honor drops
desultory threads of moss all scratchy
lines the beard of Alexander

THE OWL AND THE CLOUD

Roberto Calasso said there were nine
owls in the frontispiece
but the ninth is just an eye
emerging from the feathers of the third

six stand on the plinth in a parasitic crush
with a seventh hunting

in this impression nothing
appears on the plinth
but lines of static
or casual shadow
in what Calasso calls uncanny light and previous
scholars say is weakness
in handling the acid

the tree in front is the most
fertile in the etchings
it does not spread out
there are rings of leaves
parasitic lush
and hung with moss

owls clutch the textless
stubbly stone
waiting for Tiepolo
to claim his work

scholars note
two owls stare out

I love the one who turns his back
and wills a cloud
                    this is a way
of willing distance to infinity
the shaky line is Tiepolo's
concession to the owl

THE SHRINE OF THE LATER SIBYL

so you wanted to hear what a sibyl sounds like you human
animals you mock
my ode to the hatchet and my wrapping
paper but I've fed
greater magicians than you to my altar I've planted
my owl between your leader's legs
and you know what that means
Amiri Baraka says whoooooo
who who who whoooooo
that's not what you thought a sibyl sounds like
ok for the faint
boy with the quiver I commend you
to the marriage of Cadmus and Harmony
peace on earth the marriage
of Cadmus and Harmony peace
on earth you think a profoundly
original language wouldn't kill
the rest of you through your beardy
ears you're mistaken my hatchet
has sliced Medusa's
face off this shield you've got nothing
on your pillow for the altar
caricature Tiepolo asid
raja Qoheleth heilig
balikbayan orior
forensic science hen kai pan
the dream surrender of Peru

THE BIRTH OF FANTASIA

the other apprentice is boy and pregnant by
hisandherself confirmed
since the snake rose from its urn our master
hasn't chanted for years but waits
spreading his lap his face
drooling and dark
as when someone wants something the jaw
forgets his jaw forgets his desire
tilts his pose it
illustrates the perfect
orthogonal of his time
without expected torque its
torpor stops torque

and still the snake rises

Master has forgotten he waits for the infant
born of one fertile
hermaphrodite
he's obsessed with his owl
waking in alchemy
of skulls and codex and battle-flagged trumpet

my task is to wait in the rear with our sign
the true living snake
beside the Chaldaean
Tiepolo monument
which is real though another
Tiepolo appears where Fantasia ends
on the bottom

Tiepolo invented
this game of Fantasia
for fragments of a frieze he found
the more he reconstructed it the more
the outlines wouldn't fit
he etched them apart
the original frieze showed a famous surrender
the noblest surrender
no serpents
no owl
one bent neck
no jaw

ANGELA GHEORGHIU'S *CASTA DIVA*

AS HEARD IN THE FILMS OF

WONG KAR WAI

REPRESENTATIONS OF WATER

One sign of the demon is having one
iris replaced by an Aztec
calendar stone, the other dark
as the ocean at night
beside a single
light over a pier

Demon and I are in a modern
pub dressed as a shanty
Colored glass makes a seascape
with ships and the boardwalk
of a Hansa port
and of course the curvy-sharded sea

I ask with my dark eye
if glass is best for water

The demon tells me the word
"half-timbered" in German
and leads me out of Chartres
to another shore

"Fachwerk" concerns splitting
and therefore subject matter

We toast the souvenir of Chartres
and watch mist simmer
This means even winter
roads store sun
Headlights now and then
encounter its release

These are some of the things my so-called critical
eye can see
hungry stone

It's not so much time is circular as time
confuses memory with hope or fear
which often look like the future

I love the clear
dark between mainland
and island

The lighthouse occasionally sounds
like complaining
The rare pure
dark is the demon's
consolation
and is terribly sincere

LOVE GRANTS ME A SECULAR EUCHARIST

I've never heard so many engines
I usually don't let ears enter hearts
They sound like birds too early for spring
That is my favorite aspect today
You're fickle then *There are so many*
birds that freeze to death Why not birds
destined to live
                  but I know the answer to that
Why did you look for academic
articles after reading a poem
I am myself studying the Eucharist
in my heart *In your heart*
which tastes of cinnamon
Better spice than aluminum
Engines and birds are not made
of aluminum I see
              they are seeds
Love I have my epaulettes on
Is it the 1980s
No the immaterial epaulettes
I am your scourge etc.
Scourges do not jest
Sounds like helicopters
on land sea and air
I've given you the ears of land sea and air
Good music I will fight for you
Pilot
Pilots are seeds
I take it
you've already eaten
I've already eaten

TERROR CRATYLUS NELSON

I operate alone
Homeland Security gives men jobs
How will we get out of China
The man at the Burger King on Northern
asks where my cab is
I say I know how to walk
but usually hire a palanquin
I want no sauce but extra cheese
Like many ninjas I move in cloud
It peacocks from my taxis' rear
Elsewhere the mutation of fast food
inside Port Authority
powers the mutation of smart rats
My militia
When we counterhack China
My shelter-in-place is your shelter-in-place
I fight also for a security
producing
a new corpus for the new worms
Feed deep eep upon emergency
In the perfect language there are no puns
no metaphor no meteorology
no meter fixed slang no images
Self-sufficient = cannibal
and I am the fattest cannibal

I AM (NOT) A SCHOLAR

I trust roads and throats
to leave
out
whole forests in Prussia
Is there anywhere the walls would creak
only with meaning I could trust
I treat like a child
I must empty
I cannot cite
circa 1570
strange year of no treaty
I live in
the long night of no treaty
performing border patrols
Nowhere
Stuntbikes
Caged unicyclists power the servers
Their unitards are extreme
Mourning fire escapes
Infinite war
Tag my pelvis
I'll surrender
All and nothing
I have never died in a library

WHEN I FINISHED WRITING THIS
THE PIGEONS WERE GONE

Pigeons are beasts
They chill on their usual roof in the snow
with satellite dishes
and move less than they would if it weren't snowing
This one pigeon must be infested
because it's eating its armpit repeatedly
and slowly
hence not to keep warm
I'm also confused about how near
the songbirds' chirping is
because it's really snowing
Total beasts
There's a discussion about death in my newsfeed
Everyone assumes when you die the self dies
Of course I argue even though I agree
Wouldn't we lose so much more than our selves
that talking about losing the self
made no sense?
Nothing's accumulated yet
of the snow
The more it snows the less the pigeons move
Last week someone said I was probably too young to
    feel mortality
so I ran around a cemetery
and concluded I agree
but notice when you really watch beasts standing still
you end up staying stiller than the beasts
Along the row of cop-cars lining the tombs
past the sanitation plant
the sidewalk ended near the BQE

I ran on the shoulder over fresh-looking trash
The plastics said Contain me please contain
me please pick me
up and I

LOVERS DON'T READ KAFKA

I'm too busy to do anything but be in love
attempting meditation on a train and all
I got was a hot pink line
many possible frictions of metal on metal
it's like the only metaphors we have for things'
coming together are symphonies and fucking
we were at Storm King
Sculpture Center
the water
grass
was eating your shoes
underneath a gong in its great metal chamber
a puddle shook independently
gonggg I want to fuck a symphony
into you gonggg
gongg gongg gongg gongggg
my body muscular
and round as a drive-thru
the simultaneous power and disconnect
of blooming weeds
I want to give these flowers
the flowers of the Annunciation
to you
the whole room
a red canopy
a dark wood bed
a fire
a fan
since you're ready to read poetry
Kafka said the Messiah
had already arrived

in paradise one cannot read Kafka
I have never read Kafka
the supervirginal color is blue
you must believe
all women and brown folk
on the inside are blue
and the poem will give you a brown vagina
and this blue room
let's all be alone in the same blue room
at the same time
let's close our eyes
let's choose the afterimage
a puddle yes
no one cleans in paradise

OCCUPY WALL STREET

Let's imagine workers drinking
on their hands and knees or bent

Bruegel was also making a joke
where haystacks resemble their laborers

Like any other buffet, a panorama
isn't about infinity

Bruegel dutifully
makes the church big but cuts it off
Middleground branches unevenly
frame and cover it
the way they'd cover the genital shame
of Adam and Eve: the point is

there's really only one option here
Contrary to popular scholarly views
of landscape, you don't
own what you see, nor
does it own you: instead
color promises patterns in time

The present is gold
The past on that other hill, too, gold
It's not dumb to say hay is gold
here at the birth of capital

so Bruegel was carting it out of an old
painting by Bosch where drunks
and other fornicators

ride a monumental
haywagon to hell

Here Bosch's wagon's stripped to just gold
Let's say it travels perpendicularly
between the golden hill we left
and the golden present
toward the village green

where very small citizens throw sticks at birds

Let's go back to calling gold hay
and observe the stick-and-animal games it funds

Meanwhile the workers are drinking
There's one jug left, which we've hidden in the hay
But our buddy's coming with another
and a black jug of water

Once there were six of these paintings
Bruegel saw calendars of seasonal labor
and imagined them as panels on a wall

originally in Antwerp
now mostly in Vienna
This in New York
has the best and warmest panorama
for this most profitable season

I'm talking to you
It's harvest-time now
and there are many dead empires in this painting

Bruegel signed it in fake Roman in the corner
on a fragment of presumably ancient wall
Beside him workers line
their stomachs with bread
Look at them
He wants us to hear them eating

He wants the worker's scythe
to bend our nostalgia-
path through the hay

to this central event in the creation of profit

The hero's possibly passed out drunk
He splays his legs like the haystacks he makes
We must not submit to be measured in gold
This is what snores through his four dark teeth

hard to miss the flies asleep
on the walls come in
from winter
since it gets

just semi-dark and I
only partially
alone for the walls
conduct the neighbors

and yet each night
there is one
sweet second my phone

brightens and my chest
brims up
to my eyes
till I see

it's half
past midnight and only
linking arms
with a satellite

which I foreseeing my phone
returning to dark
told you once in the Armory
were the first things I'd save

satellites

　　　and with
a city atlas
I murder
the flies

GOOD NIGHT

THE MAD EXPANSE

There are probability-based theories that aliens
should have already arrived.
There are conspiracy theories that aliens have.
No one seems to have encountered
my better theorem (which supplants Kardashev): that
the energy required
to support any life we'd recognize
while simultaneously propelling it
past the gravitational pull
of the solar system
of a planet capable of supporting
any life we'd recognize
would drain the planet and reave it
of its capability
to support any life we'd recognize

and furthermore the Mad Expanse
effectively without gravity
isn't space at all
but something so transformative
it reaves time
and (I think u better recognize)

I

slept on a bed of nudes again,
huddled nudes, huddled in gymnastic tucks
after up
a night listening
to the lamp

and returning to the flesh, its Easter palette,
hurt my teeth: I'm asking you
what should a person accomplish in suffering

or accept arms around you, saying
the project of dawn
looks
like the project of twilight and

happily

several languages attest
to energies of light: so they must
exist, one's own arms

a cave of it

I

created misty battlements
to come in time
of siege as myself

an amazed castle

or I have arrived many festivals
later under
a harpy moon

and before it
I do not hide but amazed
of this heaven black
of feathers and someone
or you
peeking between crenellations
are heating a stripe
of iron not
to make it sharp
but infinitely sharp
the first
wire

I

found the trumpet taller
than the angel and lean
as a flamehead: now

the city burns and the bend
in the slickfaced harbor
blinks, now bulwarks

left behind against the brown
gasoline sea
my ankles wade

a nude man strung
alive through the several
strings of a harp
teaches his guardian monster

I

stayed up the shortest night of the year to greet the monster
Summer
dear monster

you softened the beasts of the glade
with a stare that I ran
with sun-coming sounds and they only

looked up as I
with your stare in their dawn
and twilight
sidelong faces
with

those greens that are almost purple that are
the dewpoint was unstill

the animals of you
inside that tideturned
color and I
inside the mostly silent
paces
agreed to prosper
of that hour

WHITE WEDDING SONNETS

IT'S A NICE DAY TO START AGAIN

It's a nice day for a white wedding
Necessary rivers appear funicular
as the one that leads past Florence
in Pollaiuolo's *Hercules*

and Deianeira the damage to which panel
makes it the discontinuous animal
of a less oily century
of an old humidity in which

weakness which is haggling with god
distills to a sweeter roue
which lemons at a banquet
even undrunk

cannot compete with as Hercules
aims at the centaur stealing his wife

HEY LITTLE SISTER WHAT HAVE YOU DONE

Today a frost light
rules all hated creatures
among which one incessantly
aims at the centaur stealing one's wife

One cannot compete with/as Hercules
Driving east one does not tell the weather
which lemons at a banquet
to savage or hail

Met by the rumblestrip
one inquires beyond it politely
of a less oily century
What is your animal life?

No labors appear
in Pollaiuolo's *Hercules*

IT'S A NICE DAY TO START AGAIN

Driving east one told the weather
to stew and the other asked
"What is your animal life?"
and "What kind of strife

rules the beloved creature?"
One claimed "Its being in our organs
makes it a discontinuous animal"
and the other "Our organs

could be the kind residue
of an old humidity" in which
weakness which is haggling with god
distills to a sweeter roue

Even undrunk
necessary rivers appear funicular

IT'S A NICE DAY TO START AGAIN

One of us demanded a wedding
of an old humidity in which
to stew, and the other asked
that clam shacks on the isthmus

distill to a sweeter roue:
and what kind of strife
even undrunk
drives east and tells the weather

to match its catenary dew?
One claimed its being in our organs
could be the kind residue
of the Other our organs

obscure. The other collected
hygrometers and waited

LOOK FOR SOMETHING LEFT IN THIS WORLD

What is your animal   life
Asks your wagon wheel while you
Aim at the centaur stealing your wife
It could be a kind   residue

That makes you a discontinuous animal
While the centaur dissects her
According to esoteric sagittal
Rules   the beloved creature

Performs a last dance with her tether
Of weakness   which is haggling with god
Driving east you tell the weather
Gentle please on the temple façade

That will depict her
Where necessary rivers appear funicular

THE BEAUTY MARK IS INFINITELY DEEP

. .

too much pain
why does the unconditional
supposed to be immediate
I keep harming   a temple
absolute contingency
if you join me we'll all be radically

tirami radically free

Rosalind Franklin
Watson apologized
the tobacco mosaic virus
you got in cuneiform
get up
the end
is happy
facts and or
language we never read

. .

get up
the beginning
I was doing
the magic look
at my enchanted life trick
again not even
drinking with tiny
Muslim girls wanting
my number not knowing
I'm too [passing?] to help
let me tell you ten
how   nope

I had silver instead of college
in my eyes
medieval Italian
worth of silver now tell
the mosquitoes arsenic
all fucking night I'll give you my email
now gather round because we won't be friends
and oh please never
look me in the eye
make sure I know
you don't want to be my lover your mother
came back into your dreams to say
I'm stunningly beautiful
modest not Muslim
in bed
a phone

. .

try not to speak unless someone is wrong

a haze over Manhattan
a summer
cold train
I just image-searched "peignoir," and late
ways to have a body
purple sky
pre-fab buildings   old ivy
floating on our eyes
hairs on a slide of the central park
of the garden of earthly delights

(meanwhile
across the room in the triumph of death)

cold ride starry
cold ride starry 7
train what happened when you called the past a hangover
do you apologize
that's a waspy way to look at drinking
I will never get drunk on time

• •

it's not just a cliché   Satan
was in fact the most beautiful
porn Fabionic
the better maker
better love what have I learned from Cori
copp the men
I would not date
historian the
artist of forgetting
against the renaissance against
antiquity   Ariadne
abandoned
I said
I wanted
to marry Nietzsche I meant
I am the wedding let's
be real be
come the wedding
pull the graying tiger lily
stems cold sunrise more than bifurcated
tips

I was online in another world
with the phrase
"forensic science"
a fucking wreck
clues turned to gold
divers food-
stuffs   parallel
incessing   fallen
navel   my yacht
was called

THE DREAM OF THE WHISTLEBLOWER

Ten dead deer
Sacrifices
Along a fracked
Susquehanna
Then
A living doe
Watched an open
Bar over Rochester
The humans
Tamed the moraine
With Art Deco
And my sagging tits
In Missoni
Responded
Two whistles
Then more
Dirt

much later woke beneath the albedo
the variant
gendered moon
a sacrifice
rhinestones on Bill Belichick
on Halloween all times
come up whole
the beauty mark is infinitely deep
that was a pimple and I
terribly allergic
drawn
wherever water has lived
reply, staghorn sumac tea
apotropaicon
not prophylactic
invitation

• •

too much pain / I believe you can have [what you want]
why unconditional / where [what you want] is continuous
infinite
over a non-linear range of time

To believe desire must go without
answer = to privilege
the male orgasm
telos and nothing
a denouement, the sword
tumbling at the gate

Srsly [we] cd always be coming
where [we] are not subjects
of an appended penis

Do not fear my boundless pleasure
That lizard in the styrofoam
The hammock, someone's
Chicken fingers
The Renaissance art historians' mojitos
Where Italy is a 19th
Century opera
About Matthias Grünewald
Max Ernst and Aristarchus
Tenor countertenor
where it is no longer efficacious
to separate being from becoming

To my beautiful mathematician
in Berkeley or in Bangalore
I called when I got a position
I live near Detroit

MAX WEBER'S *THE PROTESTANT ETHIC*

AND THE SPIRIT OF CAPITALISM

(TR. TALCOTT PARSONS)

NO KNOWING

That a really accurate calculation or estimate may not
exist, that the procedure is pure guess-work, or simply
traditional and conventional, happens even to-day in
every form of capitalistic enterprise where the circum-
stances do not demand strict accuracy.

I have recurring
dreams that unreadable blisters
are growing out of my skin
then on Roosevelt Island
I had to ask Megan if the water was dangerous
before I believed it, the breach
of saltwater over and over
on New-Englandine rocks
calling swimming swimming out
touching my eyes
small suns and television
treasure or teeth
the coming summer perhaps
the flowers dying directly
end up back in the leaves
if the roots work the way they're supposed to
and the wind isn't too redistributive
no knowing
how optimism started in the flowers
and ripened with them too I fell
for a powerful charlatan
into a future the flower-parts
smelling better flattened
that Dickinson poem with the bubbles
the charlatan my self

those days
when history has been erased between
today and a particular past
I've thought of beauty as straight-up
fullness the rich
guano in a parking garage the open
hall of its foyer with concrete stairs
scaffolding its side
old
black
slime deposits agglomerate to gumslops
and isn't it
a gray cool cavern that connects the worlds
literally here between car and sun
but any worlds, self-slaughter and rose
was I restless watching MTV
those open summers interlocking
Minesweeper and the gun cabinet
I learned "writers' block" from the internet
a wall-to-wall carpet
pink it was possible
to hide things there
a notebook under the backcushion
of my father's chair
careful
charts of biblical genealogy
knotting the first pages
so no one would check the rest
one day
I will make the twenty-eight
hours of travel to Jellyfish Lake
as an offering for what I survived
elsewhere

a lagoon of jellyfish
rising before dawn when unwitting I
dove into them and swam to the jetty
should have killed me
I was also moving for the sun
a healthier algae on the rocks a prickly
resistance from the coral
blooming venom in my feet
I've got to keep working through this
saying
slime everywhere incorrectly
appears like health
if not then don't write poems
I'm waiting for the lavender dove
to afternoon my window
it comes regardless of my hunger
which I submit if trained prepares for love

MELENCOLIA II

[T]he feeling was never quite overcome, that activity
directed to acquisition for its own sake was at bottom
a *pudendum* which was to be tolerated only because
of the unalterable necessities of life in this world.

now and then I measure fertility
with a soft tape measure I bought
to measure fertility
in terms of horizontal
sections of my body
in the last dream blisters
appeared on one side of my vagina
but I didn't look inside
I woke to the bus
Georg Simmel totally called it
the city replaces my presence
but he got the valence wrong
it is soothing as a river
I have never bathed in a river
I think of my body as a hulking
force for abstraction
thus cannot admire Cézanne's bathers
except as staging my donation
of my body to modern art
which I don't want to do
I do not want to stand against the river
I want to take the pressure off
being here, let's be honest
my righteous life has been leaving the note
admittedly a happy human note
this is what I think the putto is doing
making something human

in Dürer's *Melencolia I*
sitting on a millstone
some say comes from Plato
I first learned it from Cézanne
in the 1890s, the perfect
palette and a possible
future in the colors
around a blankish millstone, I still value
that perfect naiveté
I remember the Barnes Foundation
Merion Pennsylvania
Harry made us the reservation
he looks the same today
I was a kid
with only a couple years of museums
I thought art was not about money
I thought art history was not for the rich
so there I started
scribbling away, post-human
attribute of something greater
and sadder, gigantic Melencolia
industrially girdled and grumpy she can't
compass her lap nor its required
drapery, meanwhile me
a balding baby, independent
but with wings related to her wings
gathered sleeves and ankle pudge
recalling her bulk's bulge and her gown
and unlike her
productive: that's me
I am just a sidekick
I am finally the sidekick
of someone worthy of me

THE MOSS OF THE DANUBE SCHOOL

To speak here of a reflection of material conditions in
the ideal superstructure would be patent nonsense.

recurring dreams should mean something haunts me
I was trying to identify the two men standing
in the background of Holbein's
Noli me tangere
a younger man guides an older man
who reaches in the composition
beneath where the Magdalene reaches for Christ
not as thwartedly as she
probably in another time
and testament
I saw our hands touching like the gloved
hand of the gambling
woman in *2046*
black lace against a slit-gowned hip
I told you not much haunts me
Dürer's hands in the Thyssen-Bornemisza's
Christ among the Elders: the elders
stand in the dark
not much history around
a hat with Hebrew letters on the side
but in the center
two gnarling hands and two
hands of the youthful Christ
I'm overfull
because I see these four hands over and over
what could Holbein's younger man
deny his lover
or his father, indicating
a long road to the city below

while to the right the cloven
toe of one angel
inside Christ's tomb
the angel has daintily exposed
strange angelic part
in Queens a thunder
of public transportation
and a fountain nearby that sounds like rain
do not touch
I collected all the images I could find before the internet
became a database occasion
of *Noli me tangere*
Titian, Fra Angelico
even Correggio in the year 2000
not Holbein
it's a kind of ugly painting
got something of his father's
fifteenth-century
German dollface on Christ and something
proto-pan-European in
the drapery and space
I got it in an email from London
the day after I willed
my hand grazing yours
let it happen then I turned it
and grabbed yours and eventually
you took yours away
Holbein was really careful too
even the trees in his *Noli* aren't parallel
and definitely none of the legs or arms
not the old man's staff
there are too many crosses for a convincing
Golgotha and the foreground
lawn recedes too well

a blade of grass over Christ's good toe
there's no wind in the foreground but where the old
    man reaches
the wind blows behind him his two-toned cape
yellow and white
color of Easter trumpets
the wind
blows the youth's thin hair into mountains
and everything distant, the city
has thinned itself
in the copy I got via email
it's hard to tell if the white overall
is damage or varnish
I'll go with varnish
archaeology is easier than addition
if you believe in getting things right
there are many textures of gray in this rain
Cézanne liked to relate himself to Moses
shown the promised land
and never permitted
now for Moses, never permitted
the trees remember the moss in Germany

THE DESPERATE EARTH

If any object can be found to which this term [spirit of
capitalism] can be applied with any understandable
meaning, it can only be an historical individual, i.e.
a complex of elements associated in historical reality
which we unite into a conceptual whole from the stand-
point of their cultural significance.

I had many dreams after finishing the whiskey
and forgot them all once they made me sober
a quiet tower the small
plant from K-Sue
blooming straight up and indifferent to Manhattan
where the sun comes from each afternoon
who she asked *is a native* and the answer
hurt me
a series
of embedded dreams embodied
in one body after another the toylike
breasts of the nude
grow from my left ankle
where drapery ends in the bust of a merchant
from my hand a head mixing an ancient
orator and satyr and highest
rising from my back
a young man museologically a youth
anointing my nude with Mary Magdalene's can
the merchant's
beard in my hair
I am interested in the pornographic
loinscrap I wear as Dürer's
sogenannter *Desperate Man*
one of only three etchings

only my clothing
in waking life
marks my nativity
which is flexible
in Queens my shapely
sturdy legs draw whistles for themselves
I think Dürer's hands must have wanted to etch
to try it and the pleasure
was not sufficiently interesting
so all we have is this
series of hangovers
series of possible persons in a bodily
relation the torment
of the desperate man is the possibility
of being the nude, the merchant,
the politician as satyr, youth, no, the presence
of that possibility, the unrelenting
presence of possibly someone else as self
oneself as more than accident of birth
I think of K-Sue in the western canyons
of this country
the United States
a nativity crèche of some wild west
would feature only one person
why not her
what am I wearing anyway
what is she wearing
I love her for trying to wear the Earth
as all possible habitable planets
today I will try to wear the Earth
as all possible habitable planets

Aim at the Centaur Stealing Your Wife
© 2015 Jennifer Nelson

ISBN 978-1-937027-51-3
Distributed to the trade by Small Press Distribution
www.spdbooks.org

Design by Last Nights Sandwiches
Typeset in Baskerville and Devanagari Sangam MN

Printed and bound by McNaughton & Gunn, Saline, MI
Covers printed letterpress at UDP on paper from Mohawk
Paper Company, Cohoes, NY

Interior images are from Antonio del Pollaiuolo's *Hercules
and Deianira* (ca. 1475-80), which appears courtesy of
Yale University Art Gallery

First Edition, First Printing 2015

Ugly Duckling Presse
The Old American Can Factory
232 Third Street, E-303
Brooklyn, NY 11215
uglyducklingpresse.org

Funding for this book was provided in part by a generous
grant from the National Endowment for the Arts

ART WORKS.

National
Endowment
for the Arts
arts.gov

Some of these poems first appeared in the following magazines: 6x6, *The Atlas Review*, *The Baffler*, *Bling That Sings*, *Broken Toujours*, *The Death and Life of American Cities*, *Forklift, Ohio*, *Handsome*, *No, Dear*, and *Sand Journal*.

Some poems also appear online at *Ink Node* and in the *Occupy Wall Street Poetry Anthology*.